Engineers Work with Gears

Richard Tan

Rosen REAL READERS

Rosen Classroom™
New York

Engineers use math and science. They make **tools** to help us.

Engineers use many tools. Gears are a tool that they use. Gears have teeth called **cogs**.

Cogs have spaces between them. The cogs of one gear fit into the openings of another gear.

The gear on top looks like a **screw**. The bottom gear looks like a wheel with teeth. When the bottom gear moves, the screw turns.

Gears make watches work. The cogs fit together and move the gears.

The gears move the hands on a clock.

Clocks without hands don't use gears.

Mills use gears. As they turn, the millstone moves and breaks **grain** into small pieces.

Watermills are gears. Water moves the wheel. The wheel moves the gear.

The wheels of this train are gears. The cogs fit the track. This helps the train move.

This girl's bike moves using gears, too. As she pedals, the gear and chain move the wheels.

Glossary

cogs The teeth on a gear. Cogs allows a gear to move another gear.

grain Any food crop, such as wheat, barley, or rye, that is related to grass.

screw A metal pin with a metal thread or ridge that goes around it in a spiral.

tool Something that helps people do a job.